Math Counts

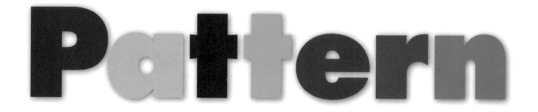

By Henry Pluckrose

Mathematics Consultant: Ramona G. Choos, Professor of Mathematics

Children's Press®

An Imprint of Scholastic Inc.

This game board is made with black and white squares.

The squares are laid out in a regular way.

They make a pattern.

This board is also made with black and white squares.
They are not laid out in a regular way.
They do not make a pattern.

Patterns are all around us.
You can find patterns in nature—
on the heads and petals of flowers,

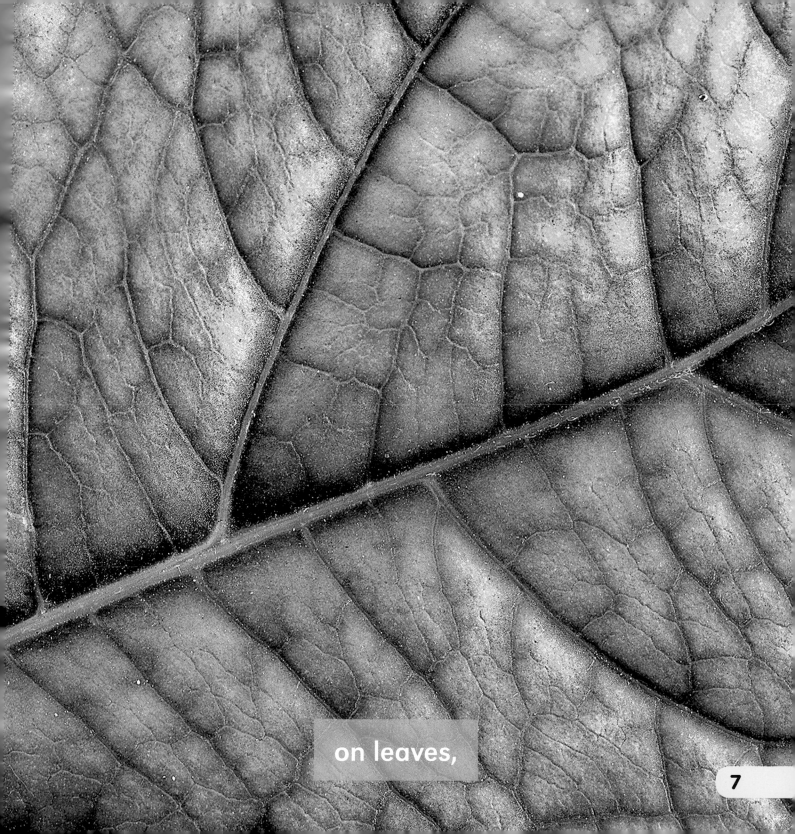

on leaves,

on birds,

and on butterflies.
Is the pattern on each wing
of the butterfly exactly the same?

There is a spiral pattern on this shell

and a pattern of stripes on the coat of the zebra.

We decorate our homes
with patterned wallpaper and fabric.

We put patterned carpets on the floor.

We eat from patterned bowls

and plates.

Things we wear are
often patterned,

and so are clothes
worn on special occasions.

Many patterns repeat themselves.
Can you see the repeat in this pattern?

Some patterns repeat themselves in a different way. How does this pattern repeat itself?

There are patterns almost everywhere.
What shapes repeat themselves
in these cranes to make a pattern?

What pattern can you see in these cobblestones?

Some shapes fit together tightly
to make a pattern,

and some leave little spaces.
The spaces make a pattern, too.

The swimmers are making a pattern with their bodies.

The water makes a circular pattern
when a drop hits the surface.

This is a close-up of a car tire.
Why does it have this pattern?

There is also a pattern on the sole of this sneaker.
How does the pattern stop a runner from slipping?

Why does this grater
have a pattern?

The spiral pattern on the rope
gives you a good grip during a tug-of-war.

Look around you.

How many different patterns can you see?

Index

Reader's Guide

Visit this Scholastic Web site to download the Reader's Guide for this series:
www.factsfornow.scholastic.com Enter the keywords **Math Counts**

Library of Congress Cataloging-in-Publication Data
Names: Pluckrose, Henry, 1931- author. | Choos, Ramona G., consultant.
Title: Pattern/by Henry Pluckrose; mathematics consultant: Ramona G. Choos, Professor of Mathematics.
Other titles: Math counts.
Description: Updated edition. | New York, NY: Children's Press, an Imprint of Scholastic Inc., 2019. | Series: Math counts | Includes index.
Identifiers: LCCN 2017061285| ISBN 9780531175101 (library binding) | ISBN 9780531135198 (pbk.)
Subjects: LCSH: Repetitive patterns (Decorative arts) —Juvenile literature. | Pattern perception—Juvenile literature.
Classification: LCC NK1570 .P59 2019 | DDC 516/.15—dc23 LC record available at https://lccn.loc.gov/2017061285

Copyright © The Watts Publishing Group, 2018
Printed in Heshan, China 62

Scholastic Inc., 557 Broadway, New York, NY 10012.

7 8 9 10 R 28 27 26 25 24 23 22 21

Credits: Photos ©: 4: invizbk/iStockphoto; 5: invizbk/iStockphoto; 6: Pamela Webb/EyeEm/Getty Images; 7: taviphoto/iStockphoto; 8: Thomas Dekiere/Shutterstock; 9: Danita Delimont/Getty Images; 10: Werner Schnell/Getty Images; 11: PanuRuangjan/iStockphoto; 12: zuzulicea/iStockphoto; 13: Ayse Mardinly/EyeEm/Getty Images; 14: Sam+Yvonne/Getty Images; 15: Dave King/Getty Images; 16: Maria Mitrofanova/Dreamstime; 17: British Modern Photography/Getty Images; 18: CSA Images/Printstock Collection/Getty Images; 19: MAIKA 777/Getty Images; 20: Michael Rosskothen/Shutterstock; 21: Andrew Koturanov/Shutterstock; 22: Jag_cz/iStockphoto; 23: NS Photograph/Shutterstock; 24: Pete Saloutos/Getty Images; 25: Nacivet/Getty Images; 26: GREENWALDOS/Shutterstock; 27: Halfpoint/iStockphoto; 28: Joe Gough/iStockphoto; 29: Fuse/Getty Images; 30: oversnap/iStockphoto; 31: Manfred Gottschalk/Getty Images.